The purpose of me writing a first time book is to give myself a personal reflection and reference on my biggest achievement to date in which I can look back on later on in life and read about my experiences and lessons that I had learnt in detail.

Once in a lifetime opportunity to also inspire others of similar young age that no matter what, you should always try and achieve your dreams sooner rather than later; Tomorrow may never come, go for it Today!

I don't think there are enough people out there in the world who share their personal insights, as a lot of people are too wrapped up in what others are have to be focusing on self improvement

If I can inspire even 1% of readers by how I was able to live out my dream, then I will be really proud and happy.

Whether people see my story as a success or failure, I have no regrets on how I started and ended my first business adventure as ultimately I can always say

- "I Did It My Way"

Blessings and Love From Garcha RS

Table of Contents

Personal Statement – 1

Dream To Reality – 7

My perspectives – 14

Part I – Age Defiance – 16

Part II – Self Motivation - 22

Part III – Self Success – 28

Pre-start up - 33

Timeline - 44

Opening store - 56

Customers - 68

Eventful Engagements - 77

Suppliers - 87

Staff - 92

Public perception - 99

Competition - 105

Investors - 112

Happiness in health over happiness in money – 117

Leaving legacy - 123

Aftermath and Future - 129

Extras:-

Quotes - 138

Meanings and lessons learnt through life's experiences - 150

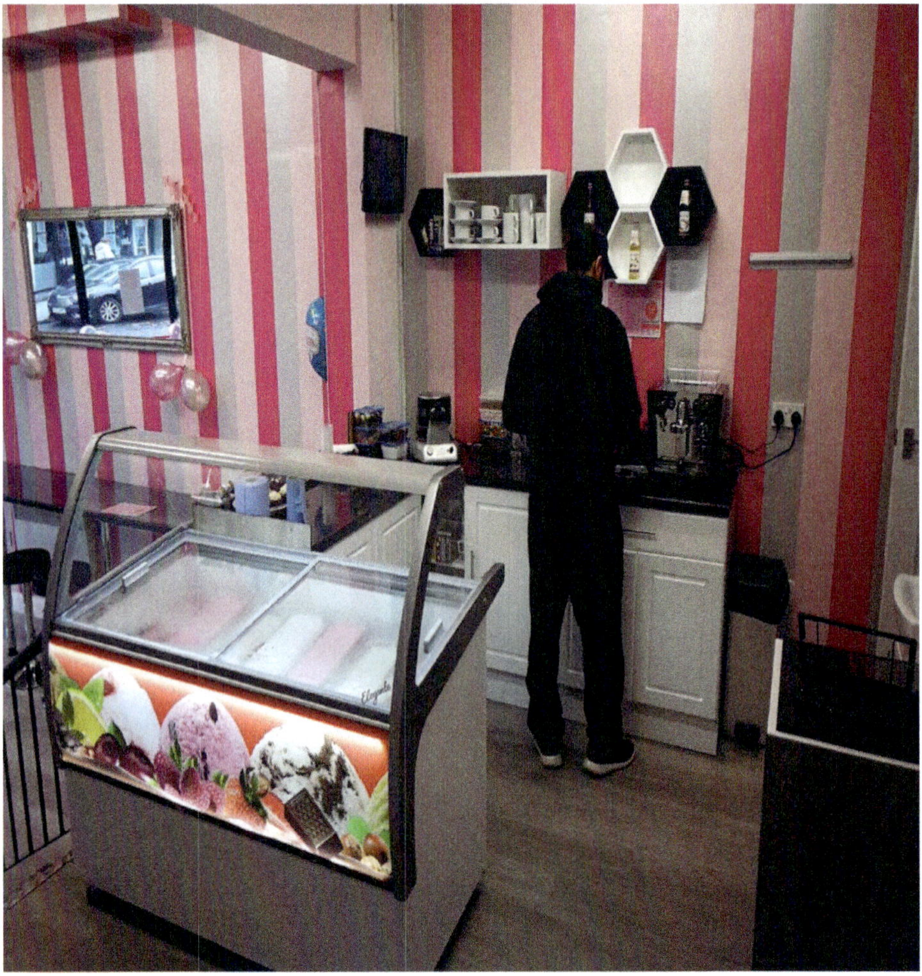

Dream To Reality

Just a young man with a big dream,

No prior business experience,

No relative industry or market knowledge,

They said it was impossible; my teachers, my neighbours, friends and family all had doubts but I have always known what I am capable of and given half a chance this was now my time.

If you are not ready now, you'll never be ready….let's go!

There is never enough time for practice, you have to travel into the unknown and work on your problems as you go along.

Nothing in life comes easy or fast, the hard work behind the scenes becomes untold by many. All we tend to acknowledge is the end result to entirely base ones successes on.

As a wise man once said, "success is not final, failure is not fatal, it is the courage to continue that counts most."

The difference between a smart one and a blessed one is that one came up with gifts and the other came down with a gift. Which one are you? Does it really matter. No, not entirely as your fortunes are just about to change, your defining moment starts now!

How are we going to know whether we can read and write if we don't start by breaking the letters down one by one and rehearsing the alphabet.

How are we going to ride a bike without falling? Of course, we have to first use stabilisers to maintain balance until we are ready to go alone.

Same goes with business, you will not know how to run a successful business until you actually put yourself out of your comfort zone. Be strong, be confident and be fearless like you once were riding a bike and learning new words and syllables for the first time.

Teachers and parents will guide you in your initial start out as a young one but then it is all on you and your resilience alone to put in the effort as you grow.

For sure you can gain knowledge as you progress throughout all academic studies, together with personal traits instilled throughout your upbringing. However, now you have to put all these factors into motion to know if your knowledge and skills were ever of any use. By any means necessary you have to do, do, do rather than say, say, say.

Our Dreams are what keeps us alive with a sense of direction to follow and envisage a new dimension in our lives. Whether this is becoming a qualified professional, owning a big house with a healthy family or albeit investing in real estate and businesses for example.

A sense of becoming to live a better, happy and more prosperous life, is what we should all be aspiring to do at any given moment in our lives. There should be no restrictions, whether it be saying you do not have enough time, money or even the skills, simply nothing is impossible.

I was not gifted with an abundance of funds to invest or valuable knowledge. I had worked hard to grow my knowledge over the many years by enduring different experiences and adapting to my surroundings while living away from home for a few years. This where I became a man who could now stand on his own and accomplish anything that I had set my mind to.

If I can do it, there is no reason why anyone else can not conquer their dreams too, if they really wanted to and believed totally in themselves. Dreams are there to pursue for a reason, nothing is handed to you in this life no matter who or what power you think you may possess.

What is it going to take? We have all a tendency as we grow older of a particular future dream whether it is something small like owning a certain car or far more audacious in wanting to become a president of an entire nation.

In order to achieve your success you have to start somewhere, perhaps working extra hours overtime to save up for a car or maybe pursuing a political related degree at university to kick-start your first step towards your big dream.

No one is going to come to your house or wake you up in the morning with a bag of money or a key to the White House. We have to put the effort in ourselves and, in the end be rewarded for all the hard-work and persistence in not giving up no matter what comes in your way to reaching your desired promised land.

However, "giving up should only be an option if the alternative is to suffer in any harms way." What is meant by this is that we should always stick to the norms and legal practices of society and not condemn ourselves to any wrongdoings just to get to the top. For example, a force of succumbing to participating in instances of illegal activities or misdemeanours.

You will ultimately suffer the consequences for such actions. For some people it is easy to sabotage others in gaining an advantage to get what they want before anyone else does. For them it may seem morally acceptable but in time justice will prevail, so we should always retain our dignity and do things the right way.

How I would sum up myself, to keep it short would be; a dream chaser, stubborn to succeed, planning out meticulously, setting no limits within, adapting to difficulties along the way to striving for perfection.

I have always continually kept pushing myself in becoming the best possible person and achieving my dreams as soon as possible. This comes with a lot of pressure I put on myself and more often than not being out of my comfort zone over the last 5 years has really emphasised my desire to succeed. I have not been afraid to accomplish anything I set before me. Maybe some can say I have peaked too early but untimely we do not know how long we have in this life so why not experience life to the fullest without regrets.

My single biggest dream was always to open and run my own business, I never really had a typical young child's dream of becoming a firefighter, policemen or builder for example. These are just a myth we was always told by our teachers and parents. The world is your oyster, with no limits that should define what you must become by peer pressure, more so by virtue of what you self dream to become.

My field and background knowledge has always been accounting and finance related due to my natural abilities in number solving and mathematics. However, I never let this limit me and now I was on a mission to achieve my upmost ambitious dream since my birth and here is how it all began to prosper from Dream to Reality.

My Perspectives

I believed that there were three parts that would ultimately lead me in turning my dreams into reality which are as follows: Age Defiance, Self Motivation and Self Success were all equally crucial in my approach.

No one should enable us to think we are too young or too old to follow our dreams. As we generally deem ourselves being respondent to others passive comments as potentially off-putting and without real context. Adamantly use this to inspire yourself to another level in the second concept of self motivation.

Self motivation is a foremost key element of understanding the will and necessary drive you possess, convene, and continually utilise in order to embark upon a sense of self success or fulfilment in any act or journey you go on in your life.

Finally, Self success is undefinable as everyone has a different perspective on what they feel contempt with in being a success or a failure in their actions. It is vital to remember and understand that as before, "success is not final, failure is not fatal, it is the courage to continue that counts".

Part I - Age Defiance

Now most young adults aged 22 are either just settling into a new job after graduating from university or they have left school early and learnt a trade for themselves to work within an industry that sets itself.

It is not about being inexperienced or lacking the maturity at a young age to consider yourself able to lead out a team in your new business for the first time. We have to inspire ourselves to be better always and live life to your full potential, start now and learn later as you proceed on.

I led a team of similar age to myself in my first business and as well as having the time of our lives, we always put work at the forefront in the culture I set to follow.

Life is short they say, now I say life is too short of real stories; we tend to be more interested in others and their success stories in the hope we could be like them achieving big things. Now question yourself and say "Why can't I be like them and enjoy my own success story?"

Age is not a defining mechanism which should deter anyone from pursuing their goals whether albeit young or old.

An unspoken amount of times we hear more often than not people decide to deter their personal goals and prolong their dreams into a later time in their lives.

This could be because they may need additional time to build on their knowledge, feel more comfortable, need support from a partner, future husband or wife or because of other personal commitments we sometimes can get too attached without reason of "no, il do it tomorrow".

Today is the day, there may be no tomorrow or day after, putting things off will only spread more doubt in the mind of your dream being impossible.

There is a well renowned saying that "if you are old enough, you are good enough." Let us transpire this into reality and subsequently reap all the rewards.

The feeling within will always have doubts and a sense of fear of failure but we will never better ourselves without acting on our mistakes when they come about.

Life will always be a learning experience which you pass on your abundance of memories and achievements to your kids and younger generations but first we must switch the light on inside and shine over our shadow of fear.

Let's start early on by surrounding yourself with different people from a variety of background origins, whether older or wiser. Learning, understanding and experiencing all cultures. This will broaden your horizon in knowledge and heighten your understanding of life relatively quickly.

Learning of the mistakes and obstacles the older generation had to comprehend is a timely reminder and reference that can guide you in preparing for what perhaps may come later on in your life's journey.

On the other hand, also what you need to be aware of now in the current times of ongoing change. Understanding the values and principles embedded within past generations is priceless and bespoke to building character from, timely boosting your self motivation to stay ahead of the rest.

More so from these life lessons, if you can understand others needs and interests, your now with added incentive to potentially change the world with your new business invention.

Furthermore, considerably bettering yourself along the way or you can sit and ponder what could have been and the idea may be acted upon by others. You will ultimately always have more regret in the latter outcome and how you then challenge your mind to deal with this, can subsequently make you feel worthless.

The misconception point of early failure before even beginning is not whether you say to yourself "oh it may not work out to anything." However, for some people the aspect of undertaking an additional headache, extra stress is a deterrent in itself but the worst aspect will be in the pit of your stomach telling you "what if" and that is not something that people will get over easy and excuses will continue throughout their lives.

For myself personally, I have always been strong minded, ambitious and brave enough to take that jump towards achieving my goals and dreams at this young age whether people see them as a success or a failure; I have no regrets and I would not be the man I am today without going through any hurdles or achievements in which I can always look back fondly and say I Did It My Way.

Just remember you can put a number on your birth certificate but you can't put a number on your potential, it is limitless.

Our clocks are ticking continuously as we evolve. As I aim to continue setting new laps, a record best lap even. I also now want you to think of this as being just another lap of your life, albeit just on another circuit.

Part II - Self Motivation

Once you realise your true value in life, you will only then be able to fulfil your goals and dreams while others will sit and ponder in disbelief.

I say the best come but once in a lifetime, this inspires me to be the best I can possibly be whether I am 22 or 50. I will set out to become the greatest at everything I wish to accomplish before me. Do you want to be the best? Simply put, there has never been a time like now.

Only awakening each morning and steering yourself to strive and to be in control of your own destiny should be at the forefront in kickstarting your mission to accomplishing your dreams.

Being stuck in an office job, moaning everyday you are unhappy and you really want to be doing something else is a clear indication of ruing your precious time and skills in a job which would replace you within a heartbeat, even with over 40 years of renowned service.

At the end of the day it is always every woman or man for themselves in a work place environment, so I would urge others to not sit around waiting for the right time as your gut is telling you that...., wait this isn't right!

I really am not interested in putting efforts into someone else's business when I can be pursuing my own dreams. That time will not come back and there may not be any time tomorrow by order of the grace of god if you're a believer.

Being in control of your own destiny is a comfort that opens up limitless opportunities of self-esteem. The purpose of this is that things are going your way and only you solely can guide and alter your perspective when in hard times or in a decision making problematics.

This position of power becomes untouchable as you can have a real sense of relief that no external persons can hinder or take away from what you are wanting to achieve or give out orders of what you should be achieving.

Baring in mind any wrongdoings and misfortunes occurring from your decision making, will bare the fruit of yourself only and deny the pin blame on others as your control diminishes.

I say there is a fine line between arrogance and confidence. Confidence in your own abilities is a necessity while arrogance only gets you so far but it is this balance between both that will determine how far you want and are able to get to.

Having overconfidence may also be seen as arrogance or being under confident you may need to become more programmatic in your approach. Balance!

As there will be many obstacles to overcome in any new business adventure, by having some sort of arrogance in handling and overcoming these situations, it will untimely put you in good stead and increase chances of success.

Do not be afraid to show your superiority especially in times of being in a leadership position where this quality can refrain any doubters who do not follow the same sense of direction you are aspiring towards.

Set the way, set the rules, set the culture, set the record straight when you need to. Be in charge, don't let any doubters become in charge of you!

As people come and go in your lifetime, some will go forward with you whilst others are left behind chasing your shadows.

Your initial success may be short lived by you as you move to chase the next bit of success, but those followers are still lost and trying to catch up with you so do not look back, keep striving forward!

I keep my enemies at arms length and my friends hand in hand. My fans soon turn to being haters with a passion but it is only this hate that drives me in gaining an advantage and rising above the envy that is shadowed before me.

No one else matters, only you alone know what path and successes you are about to achieve. Remind others from time to time that your still shining and use this as extra motivation to remain a strong standing presence in both yourself and for your business.

I have been blessed in a position to empower not only myself but along the way helping and guiding others to believe within themselves that we are all amazing and have the true potential to change this world for the better.

Just remember that self motivation above all separates the strong from the weak, in any given situation the key is to keep reminding yourself that YOU are special!

Part III - Self Success

How do we define success, is it money, wealth, assets?

Any single occurrence of success should not be the be all and end all in saying right I have done enough now. Keep going, build on that single success into a long line of success stories in both personal and professional achievements.

There is no limit, the only limit is set by yourself and can be altered and set again and again at anytime when only you decide what you can do in any attempts of yearning for more successes.

Albeit by adding another source of income or revenue stream by expanding a side of your business operations or a takeover of a competitor to dominate the market cap share.

There is always something or someone bigger and better, Apple was one of the first into developing smartphones and in time Samsung have sprung on and now battle head to head with Apple.

Ebay was a dominate online service selling anything to everything and to which now Amazon have outgrown them and other competition and established themselves as the biggest and best company in the world in their industry sector.

This shows there is never any time frame or limit to what you can achieve, the important aspect is only persistence of sticking to your ideas and believing your time is around the corner.

Whether that is Today, tomorrow or next year, patience to success is paramount for any business and will not happen any otherwise.

What is meant to be will be but in times when things are not meant to be, this will determine your understanding on eternity as nothing is forever.

Any relative success wether it be a short stint or a long period of sustained successes, one should remain humble and calm and not get carried away.

For majority of businesses it takes years and years to get established and to maintain their stance and portfolio ahead of competitors among the industry;

Businesses can not afford to even occur one error of misjudgment or even a drop in standards as it can be catastrophic and untimely lead to a quicker demise than the time it took to get to the top.

This is why everyday you have to be at your best and nothing less is acceptable.

A lot of things in life are materialistic and will eventually wear out of its condition and price tag in time. However, your priceless knowledge, elite abilities and human nature ascertained throughout your life span will always stay with you forever.

So do not let anyone say you are not doing well enough if you are driving a Ford and not a Ferrari. As both do the same simplicity purpose of travel and get you to and from where you want to be.

For some, money and welfare decides how successful that person is or was. This can be mistaken by the same person inheriting assets and wealth from family and past generations or even striking lucky in their lottery fortune.

It is not supposed to mean they actually put any effort in to making their own successes; so always be happy with what you have and never compare yourself with others wealth. It is a matter of when not if, you will be in the spotlight also story telling your successes to the world to listen.

We have idols and inspirations we look up to but let's aim to be greater and leave a legacy that is unmatched to all mankind. I am not aligned to normalcy, as I seek self success in my own beliefs that my vision and inner sanctuary is contempt with everything I ever wanted to accomplish and encounter during my short lifetime. And only then and then only will I be able to rest easy knowing I did it but ultimately I Did It My Way!

Pre-Start Up

Planning, Planning, Planning

Let us begin as we mean to go on….

They say the best come but once in a lifetime, let us leave our mark on this generation and eternity as a whole. Etch our names in unprecedented history by climbing to the highest highs possible without regrets. This is where it all starts to come into fruition from just an idea to actual substance.

Do not just say I will do this or I wish to do that, talking is cheap but doing is expensive. Those with the essential tools and skills will blemish in taking the talking to the next step of doing. Do not keep on your ideas to others, keep focused as this will only tantalising hold you back and derail any progress towards your end goals.

You can attempt to hang a picture frame on the wall, without the right tools and accuracy in measurements it will not last long-standing on its bearings. You may aswell leave your frame in the cabinet or on the flat shelf, same as any business invention plans and ideas; gather the correct tools to support your plans as quickly as possible to give a progressive and efficient starting.

Empty your mind onto paper, let your initiative blossom first and foremost. Reach your thoughts far and wide into the mind, before long determining the concept that is most probable to achieve. By no means the idea that you have to be completely comfortable with. As being out of your comfort zone at many times can bring out the best in you; realising many skills and benefits that you never even knew you possessed.

Continue brainstorming down any ideas or potential activities that come to mind, think freely, make as many notes on ideas baring any judgement as all business options are neither silly or impossible to achieve. Staying aligned to the main aspects of self-fulfilment and self motivation previously mentioned, as these can positively boost your chances of building up momentum and progression towards achieving success.

Nothing should deter you from attempting to embark on a new investment. Background, religious beliefs and culture; not being sceptical that past recent history has served many losses or failings. Anything prior is irrelevant to now. Just because you failed before in other concepts you pursued, there is nothing to say that this new idea will not be the correct one in defining your fortunes. Use your sufferings to spur you on towards a real sense of belonging. In doing so, trigger the inner will from within your safe haven to inspire changes fit for purpose in your happiness and future wealth fortunes.

Sometimes it is not always the right way to visualise what you wish or want to see, but merely focusing on what you HAVE to instil in your vision. By means of basing your infrastructure to the minimum necessity requirements foregoing the luxury aspects in organising the companies logistics, which are of course untimely going to be more costly in the inaugural start up.

A rocky road lays ahead, focusing in degrees, inch by inch like a moving tram from one station to another. Platform to platform, collecting new business resources and basic amenities along the way prior to ensuring the road ahead is clear before proceeding on to the next procurement stage.

Do not be afraid to use professional services of local establishments to help launch your first company and business location. It may prove costly initially but having strong foundations to operate out from and making sure the company is adept before business launch is very crucial.

Business Advisors can support with budget plans and forecasts. There is always a more often than not emphasis on keeping start up costs down to within a strict budget limit. However, along the planning stages, other costs to set up can arise unexpectedly so stay cautious regardless of what you and any advisors have forecasted. An emergency reserve fund to call it in this case should be held aside for safe measures.

A detailed step by step schedule should be devised between both advisor and yourself to facilitate the inauguration to conclusion stages in the planning system. This would then establish the business blueprint to follow on from.

Accountants can support in the logistics of assessing any borrowing options available, setting the company accounts and legalities in formalising the business incorporation to the relevant authorities. Also performing a series of financial functions such as a series of data analysis and tax advice to encourage and ensure a positive approach in remaining financially stable throughout the business entirety.

A well experienced lawyer onside will help advocate strong lease terms in negotiating for a commercial premises to trade from. Alongside this, the right location and surrounding businesses, including public, should all be well researched before any final decision is made to set up a hub. Pay attention and stay protected to any landlord misdemeanours while enacting on a lease agreement.

The base of all happenings, ins and outs, forward or backwards progression, hardships and prosperities will all derive from your business headquarters. Contemplate whether the portfolio of your aspirations will come to fruition in the selected location before proceeding to final set up.

Lower expectations and manage pre-cautions during initial stages in planning and preparation. Safeguard your business strategies from any possible sticky points that are addressed when carrying out public surveys and questionnaires. Use these findings as a starting point in monitoring the likelihood of frequency in customer number visits and potential volume of other local residents who can be targeted henceforth.

You will now start to feel a bit more reassured and comfortable in knowing that there are actual potential customers available who have indicated an interest in what you are offering in terms of a goods or services establishment.

A well established business will always firstly require strong foundations in order to maintain a smooth running of all its operations. The last thing you want to do is to start making wholesale changes to the main interior layout and altering fixtures and fittings shortly after opening as this can be very damaging to the businesses potential to strive and survive in the initial starting out phase.

To make sure you get the best possible start, you will need to have a thorough blueprint set in stall to predominantly follow. Certain aspects of the procuring process for example could involve outlining a themed paintwork colour/s for the makeup of interior walls, acquisitions of decorations and artworks to give the place a unique look. Lighting and music systems to enhance the mood and experience for all guests, furniture and fittings for guests to be seated comfortably and to match the overall theme colours and design.

Just by undertaking this fundamental approach, you would now have descended a long way down in establishing an effective base to commence business operations from. Any extra minor changes or movements of fixtures can be altered at a later time, on popular opinions from customer feedback after opening for instance.

A vigorous detailed plan would before all else need to incorporate a head title which is affectively your new business premises name sign to finish off all the procurement process in advance to the grand opening.

I myself wanted to entice customers in, to which I set vibrant, quirky colours and a simple worded front shop sign display to gain initial attraction. This worked a treat as guests would more often than not walk in for a further look at what we do and sell. Once they were inside it was now myself and my teams time to shine in our efforts to drain their wallets on our products as much as possible. Of course, I am just joking but we will get onto customers and guests a bit later on.

A well knit business is not only solely reliable on the owners; staff and management are fundamentally vital in the longevity and viability of a business as a whole. Those who follow the policies and procedures to the T, both with precision and consistency at all times will flourish in meeting both personal and company objectives set in a timely manner to stay ahead of competition. Employees and management will also be covered in more depth in time to come.

A pre trial run day if you want to call it that, I had purposely set up a family and friends evening to gather initial feedback and identify quickly any areas for improvement a few days prior to opening my first business trading day.

It is always practical to have the team of staff alongside you, just as it would be on any normal operating day. Here, any feedback from friends and family members can be acknowledged as they will have a keen eye on all the ongoings to report back upon close of the trial day.

Furthermore, I gathered I would need to give all employees a further opportunity of training for a few days but also praising their abilities to adapt swiftly to our first face to face customer engagement and service experiences. A delay to opening day was now inevitable but our systems and processes all needed to be precise and consistent in preventing any unnecessary disturbances down the line.

Of course, training is and should always be seen as on-going. I myself, am still learning all the time and new traits reveal themselves and face up to the reality of different situations as we interact with different types of customers. So we have to always be ready and willing to learn and improve on our skills.

The main feedback from the trial run was the disjointed approach in taking all table orders at the same time and then making one food item at a time to different tables in succession. This was a simple but very important aspect to get right and thus I implemented a further review of our training methods to now manage order taking and service on a first come first serve basis. All customers at any one given table should have their food and drinks served appropriately in a simultaneous order.

Quality over quantity should be at the forefront of all business practices at the starting phase. As this is essential as customers will not mind waiting a few extra minutes and thus enjoying products to the best quality you can output.

Another reason for extra training for all employees to instil within them that our high quality approach is paramount. Just bare in mind that excess training without real means and proven results is highly costly and time consuming. To avoid this, really do monitor and document all training steps and results as they are produced.

Next I will highlight a brief timeline and in-depth account of the whole process from procurement of an idea to opening the store for the very first time.

Timeline

The following is an insight on the stubborn like nature and persistent dedication needed within yourself in order to have any chance of turning your concept idea into a reality existence. It takes a long while to build up a base and enough courage to stand alone in living out your dream; whist enjoying every moment that comes with it.

- **September 2017 - The Quiet Beginning**

My recent background entitled working in the Accounting industry, a relatively large American firm based in Coventry. My time there was short lived as eventually my team was made redundant. Soon after we received our redundancy dues, I was free to explore other opportunities. I quickly saw a gap in the local town market for potential new business openings and started to timely plan what I could open as a business; which was a dream that I always aspired to experience since a young age.

A few ideas to mention were that of an Indian fruit and veg shop/stall as there was very limited choices as you had to travel far and wide out of town to get similar produce. Another option was an Indian sweet, snacks and samosas shop; also have to travel far away to buy these items. A bar and social club like pool/snooker with a relaxing bar area but I opted against any alcohol related business at this early stage as it would bring too much confrontations and nuisances as some local bars and pubs have to deal with week in week out. For a first venture this was seen as the most high risk opportunity.

The option I went for was a Dessert Parlour as this was a market currently booming nationwide and my local town never had anything of the sort, so why not go for it. I possessed currently no real industry or business experience; no previous cooking courses or even a long term interest in desserts other than to just eat them for a sweet tooth.

AIM was to simply put my wisdom and skills and experience a dream of running my own business. So now, having established the first step of achieving that dream and realising my ambition; I knew that even being out of my comfort zone, I would soon be capable of doing anything once I put my mind and focus onto it.

- ## October 2017 - Premises Search

I now started the search for a premises location and booked a few viewings. I assigned a business advisor who helped with initial planning stages and offering professional guidance. I also spoke with accountants and solicitors for the fundamental legalities needed in setting up my company. Tastebuds was the first name that came into my head when I sat for only just one minute to think of a name. I stuck with this as it was my initial gut feeling that the first name idea was the one I should proceed with.

The premises was then located in the local town parade. There was still works continuing on the rear property extensions. I was told there was around 10-11 other people also interested in the premises but I already knew the landlord from previous and discussed my idea and plans briefly to which he was happy. I knew I had time to continue planning in depth whilst building works continued but I also wanted to keep the landlord at my side closely while others were interested so I did not miss out on this prime location.

- November 2017 - Solo or Partner

I had just kept following my initial gut first thoughts on anything when it came to planning and writing ideas down. This way I felt that I would be happy and maybe make less errors in overthinking and putting things off. Family and others were reluctant for me to proceed with opening as there was doubts on whether I would be able to handle everything on my own.

I had thought of introducing a fellow business partner with similarities and some experience in the dessert industry but at the time there was not many options that overwhelmingly persuaded that I needed a partner. I had felt that my methods and decisions would become disrupted and in-turn cause delays with any partner dealings in the long run. I was not comfortable to put trust into just anyone also.

This journey was ultimately a ride for me and myself only, to go on and explore how and what it takes to be able to run a business on your own. I started to acknowledge over these months of planning that hats off to all those who have set up any business whether on a big or small scale as it was not for everyone and requires a lot of determination, motivation and persistence.

- **December 2017 - Set Up**

The company was fully set up and registered with the relevant authorities and the store menu was beginning to take shape. The suppliers were now designated and contracts set up. Business costs, prices, potential profits were all set in budgets and forecasts I produced for the first 3, 6 and 12 months schedule. Also I had to complete an online food hygiene level 2 course to build depth and understanding; and by law I needed to possess this.

The local council food hygiene inspectors would be in attendance and checking upon my opening that I understood and was in the proper conduct to operate a food business.

The heads of terms for the commercial premises was sent to us before Christmas which we looked over. I initially thought the rent was high but I had forecasted with confidence we would cover this along with other costs over time.

- **January 2018 - Lease**

Landlord began to pressure me to sign the lease and commence moving into the property but we did not favour the terms in the lease so we held various meetings and conversations to get the best terms me and my solicitor felt were necessary. Also any exit clauses or lease assignments that potentially we could have these options to use if things did not go well. In the meantime I had set up all social media pages, the final business logo, a business email address domain and staff uniforms were designed all by myself.

- **February 2018 - Operations**

Cooking equipment including utensils and cutlery were all arranged with discounts agreed and orders saved for future purchase with vendors. Furniture such as tables and chairs were also preordered accordingly to bespoke preferences. Store decor and matched themed colours, wall fittings and other decorations to enhance the interior fit for purpose, were also set out so I was ready to kit out the store as soon as I moved in. The lease was preliminary agreed to now start from March 1st 2018.

I was now in a position to start putting down action on all the plans and the talking was over, I must now deliver. In all this time, I had still kept everything close to myself and only involved those persons who were close family or friends. Only we knew between us what I was about to open. This was to protect myself from other interested parties who could potentially scupper my plans.

I do not really post or showcase on social media my personal business but now I knew I had to start sharing information on the new business about to open in the local town. This was to gain initial attraction and to start getting people talking as word of mouth is priceless for myself to seek awareness and potential customers already in waiting to try and become regular customers of ours.

My business acumen was very raw but this was a once in a lifetime opportunity to step forward and realise a dream. I now felt I had all the essentials in place to hereby put all my planning into motion.

- March 2018 - The work begins

The start, in unchartered territory a movement began. Planning, talking and visualising all came down to this moment.

Action…

It was time to put months of hard work; long hours into the night planning, forecasting and setting stones in place for this very moment. The keys were handed over to myself. I felt nervous but excited, eager but calm, focused and ready to begin the groundworks in fitting out the interior to my designed specifications.

Work began on the extended rear area where wooden flooring had to be fitted which was something I had never done before. With a little starting help from a family friend I began to work long into the first few nights piece by piece, laying the wooden floor boards down to have a solid base to work with.

There was times of loneliness and thinking whether this was going to take me forever and delay my opening plans as I worked alone through the nights. I stayed calm and remained on schedule; to start buying other painting and decorating materials to give the interior walls, ceilings and boulders a big uplift in the vibrant themed colours that became a sensation to customers later on.

Only a week into works beginning and there was already crude remarks from a few members of the public passers by, on the embarking business I was about to open. I rose above any remarks and continued with my head held aloft, knowing and believing that no one was going to stop me pursuing my dreams. Thus, I only used this negativism to propel myself and my team to really make a success in doing so.

Continuing on at pace, the walls were now coloured and decorations fitted in place. Alongside other furniture and fittings such as tables and chairs, these were all set out in accordance to a pre-set seating layout for both front and rear seating areas. Cooking equipment and refrigerations were installed and tested for smooth running operation. The main shop sign was fitted and a opening date was now set for April 11th.

Health and food hygiene inspections were all conducted and a 5 star rating was given. Much to our joy and satisfaction that now we were getting closer to opening having now gotten assurances that our systems and processes were all adequate and reliant to the just cause food business logistics.

Meanwhile, potential candidates were handing in cv's for us to shortlist the best suited to fit into our system and culture. Interviews were conducted nearby by a close trusted associate of mine and in which we duly liaised with one another on the personification and traits required by candidates in order to be successful in the roles advertised.

Soon after a review, our final shortlist was drawn out to which we then started to let our new employees know of their acceptance. Finally, I introduced myself to the new employees and expressed my intentions going forward in the pending opening of the business. Also what was to be expected from the get go with a series of training events and practices so everyone was adept and ready to hit the ground running.

Store was now set up fully ready inside and out; staff and management ready; supplies and services ready; ready or not here we come! Doors were ready to be opened for the first time soon after our trail run day.

A slight few adjustments to the internal layout were foreseen and a notice released amongst other large posters spread throughout the whole town and surrounding areas for all public to see and hear that we were about to rock n roll.

The noise was building…

Opening Store

Behold the front and back pages, headlines… "An historical moment in history, where human transcends on a journey from dream to reality."

This is what the journalists aspire to write about, causing shockwaves across the country. In the public domain, the spotlight is now shining on you, you have so far made huge progress towards your ambitions and goals which no one can ever take away from you. It does not end here however, the show goes on, let's go get it!

Don't you just love it when a plan comes together and falls in place just at the right time. The hairs are standing up, goosebumps and nerves appear for the pending opening ceremony. I stand side by side with my team ready to get started.

Be as excited as you would be opening all your presents on Christmas mornings. The difference is yourself, have now delivered a beautiful moment to transcend on without any equal. Unfasten the seatbelt, get out and upturn your horizons and chase successes. Let us not stop until you become comfortable in both self-fulfilment and wealth fortunes to provide a sense of stability to both you and your families.

It was quite a spectacle on the opening show, a much needed welcome boost to the town with a new, never seen before concept now ready for all the public to savour and enjoy alongside us. Balloons pumped, banners stamped, red ribbons were cut. I walked the red carpet for the first time in my life with my chest pushed forward, head held high, my fedora hat to the side in style with a fresh custom fit suit to match. Ladies and gentlemen, I welcome you to your new humble abode, your new hotspot, your new getaway, your new home from home.

The surrounding folklore were amazed at the fanfare going on before them and much to their bemusement at my hat, they were delighted they had a new offering at their doorsteps to now breakaway for a moment to indulge and relax.

A modern unique premises location to be seen from afar was a welcoming boost for all town residents to endeavour. I feel it is about more than just presenting a shop feature that is beneficial for visitors to update their socials with a few pictures as they pass by; our aim is that simply it is best "sometimes to just live in the moments and not cameras". What I mean by this is that we should savour more natural life moments unconditionally with our partners and loved ones.

A great pleasant, atmospheric vibe along with an adequate standard of food and products on offer for guests, is what I am accustomed to providing in terms of a quality hospitality service. However, such camera internet uploads capturing our food could be a timely bonus boost but not essential in spreading awareness of our existence. Moreover, possibly enticing others to come try for themselves.

In saying that, a continuation of our own obligations in product uploads and general marketing ploys online to all social media followers, should always be the main focal point of gaining awareness and engagements within the wider public on a consistent basis.

Business Advertising by virtue of methods such as door-door flyers/leaflets, Tv and radio announcements, online Facebook, Instagram and Google paid commercials are predominantly the most popular and effective forms undertaken. However the contingency is that any advertising ploy should be controlled and measured accordingly to get the best possible results in a timely manner.

These result findings may be worthwhile in then solely focusing on one particular form of advertising which works out best, again and again on a regular basis. For instance, say 50 customers were polled and asked how they became aware of the business and to which prompted them to try us for the first time; a simple drawn out tally chart system to track these responses could be the perfect way in highlighting the most decisive approach to pursue.

Once identified, you can now adopt more time and efforts in spending wisely as this advertising approach was bringing most success and potential earnings for the business. More future income can now be reinvested with confidence in other areas and even in the meantime money could be saved on other forms of inefficient advertising.

For example, if you was to be spending huge amounts on door-door flyering, radio announcements, bus adverts, and to of no avail were these methods working out but that of only Facebook marketing. Then, the monies spent on advertising will become way more proportionate towards Facebook marketing from here on out and rightly so.

Soon after opening the store, many other avenues were pursued to engage and build up connections with a variety of consumers. Local universities were contacted in the hope of expanding our portfolio amongst a huge network of university students and thus applying our advertising efforts within all the surrounding university halls of residences.

Hosting an event alongside the main city university was key to enacting on the desire to run various student events concurrently overtime. Keeping relations and offering unique birthday party packages in-store to enhance the enjoyment for all to participate, was fundamental to our early success.

Local schools and college marketing were also a big hit in drawing in more young adults and families. These were one of our main target audiences we identified upon initial business analysis. Posters and flyers were distributed and placed in key town areas to focus attention and drive our mission to gradually continue building up a well established customer base.

Nearby, we had a neighbouring established tuition centre which hosted a variety of learning classes throughout the midweek. My aim was to now partake in attracting more young parents who tend to spend more disposable income on treating their kids. We had a smart initiative offer set up alongside the centre whereby for every test passed by a student, they would then get a buy one get one free item from our store menu to enjoy.

You have to be brave and go seek to expand your network from time to time to remain a business stronghold and to keep up to date with all consumers trends that arise or lifestyle changes. Failure to do so, can lead to falling back and losing potential gains from exploiting the market prior to any rival competition obtaining advantages by acting out first to these transitions.

Who does not love a good party! Fiesta all the way into the night. A gathering of unique happiness to share joys and laughter with friends, families and partners. Cherishing the memories and leaving a lasting impression on the main recipient to remember forever.

Many lasting moments and memories will forever behold in my heart. Seeing the happiness and enjoyment on kids faces when celebrating birthday events was amazing. A wonderful reminder that we had just made others dream come true and now it is time for ourselves to blossom our own dreams into reality.

Seasonal periods throughout the business months were unique in their own experiences, being flexible and trying new approaches throughout first year trading is key to really understanding all aspects of consumers, local traditions and future business prospects.

Spring jump into the Easter seasons, Jesus was not the only commemorating highlight moment to be resurrected. The store tills were ringing like the church bells striking every hour. The midday mass congregated outside the doors to mark a special occasion where our sales went through the roof, it was a good Friday believe me.

Soon after our opening, our new customers were commemorating our new establishment as a testament to the towns prominence. Oh the jokes, the best thing was some employees were few and far between during this time. Some had a passover to which we became understaffed but hey it was a time of celebration right.

Popularity began to rise as our new menu items became available with a selection of waffles, cookies and puddings to mention a few. We even made an Easter egg waffle special in collaborating to the custom traditions of Easter.

Summer bliss, summer of 2018 was one of the hottest on records which came with a long lasting period of heatwaves throughout. Ice creams sales were booming of course and a far cry for us to keep supplies incoming quick enough, as high demands needed to be met consistently. This is the period we expected and acquired the most sales of our Dessert items.

Schools, colleges and universities would all be closed for the summer holidays and in which brought about a vast number increase in public footfall passing by the store. We could offer the best and coolest treats to keep the public cool from the heat and enjoy a sweet experience all at the same time. We were also the only Dessert Parlour open with a range of ice cream flavours on offer to choose from, so thus a spread of word of mouth was to be in quick succession as customers entered in and out.

It is now peak summer, the air fans are spinning fast and away, the birds are on-song, its World Cup fever everywhere. Harry Kane should have squared it to sterling…but all is okay in-store as Jeff has passed on the waffle which Rachel has intercepted and in turn whipped the cream around the waffle walls and delivered gently into the customers net for a moment of sweet sensation. The table of guests erupts in disbelief of the sighting of such pure cohesion and begin to indulge on their sweet offerings while they watch on the football. The only thing that is coming home is the tooth fairly to collect the children's sweet broken off tooth's.

The fall season, students were returning slowly back to university and schools were about to reopen again. The spooky season Halloween, pumpkins carved and lit up, spirits high in the sky, do we trick the staff or treat the customers? Dressing up in funky but scary costumes to participate in our yearly Halloween event.

Guests were invited to enjoy an evening of games and prizes that me and my team had in store for them.

Not quite monsters & martinis or Trick-or-Tequila, we saved that for the after hours party with the single parents; but more of a child friendly festival of frights which went down a treat I must say, who knew little Ben had it in him to turn our Rachel into a mummy. It was a magic trick of course for gods sake.

Celebrations now come on, its winter Christmas time season, store decorations were a plenty, behold the lights and tinsel's as the best time of the year had arrived. Tis the season to sell a lot and demand is always high for consumer goods and services, so stay on top and be prepared in advance of this vital period. Seasonal offers and discounts can be sanctioned as a gesture of goodwill to all customers with a sense of reiterating your gratitude with the support they have shown since business commenced trading.

Finally, an important aspect to consider.

When you do not have enough time to do something you want or need to do, in the time constraints that are set; you have to buy time in order to keep going and still strive towards being successful in completing your mission.

Whether it be as you begin trading from your new establishment and you need to get to a medium whereby you are breaking even as soon as relatively possible.

In attempting this, you may need to buy yourself some time, in ways of deferring potential creditors payments to longer payment due dates. Or by chasing debtors for earlier payments in advance so you are at an ease in a suitable financial standing to continue the business runnings. This will also reduce any underlying burdens that could slow progression towards your overall business objective.

Customers

Customers can make or break a business within an instance. Entirely jeopardising years of hard work and commitments in the endeavouring of a sustainable business. Establishing key customer relationships by virtue of constant healthy communications, loyalty discounts and reward systems can help ascertain a relative strong and steadfast loyalty customer base.

But nothing is certain. Customers are always looking out for the best new deals and the best new products available on the market. Other businesses can become apparent and competitive at any time so maintaining a strong-hold on your loyal customers will put you in good stead to survive initially from any future emerging competitors.

Every customer query or concern on the quality or service they have received or been receiving from the business should never be taken lightly nor matter how big or small it may be. We need to be acting fast but conscientiously in providing the necessary responses or course of action to control the situation.

Some customers do not want to engage or participate in any communication with staff, they just want to be on their way, in quickly and out quickly. Let them be, but maintain the basic principles that every business should partake in such as that of my 3 step form of PRP.

Here, every customer is unique and should be approached and received accordingly, but the basic principles of PRP are; Polite. Respectful. Punctual.

Being polite and welcoming on arrival and exit for all customers albeit whether a sit-in or takeaway order.

Respecting customers privacy at all times and giving them the upmost service of comfort and supporting their every need in making their stay a rememberable one.

Punctual in the sense to always be on hand and cautious to serve on time and also be ready to clear and tidy surfaces upon guests finishing their meals. Similar to respecting customers but making sure you are still available relatively quickly when called upon.

Are we just waiting for customers to buy from us or do we need to buy from them prior. Pinpoint your marketing strategies in enticing new customers as swiftly and at a modestly cost as possible. Sell them a dream vividly and wholeheartedly revealing complete transparency in your products and services on offer. In the process, aiming to acquire their inner rights to purchase solely from us alone rather than any other competitor/s.

Customers need to be at the forefront of any business culture and especially in the food industry. Common known fact that they spend the money to buy your goods and services which then provides you a living and untimely puts the necessities of food on your table to feed yourself and loved ones.

As a past store owner, managing relations with all types of customers on a daily basis is in fact a very challenging skill to maintain with confidence. You have to be at your best every minute and hour of the day with a smile and on alert to all situations which may occur by different types of guests incoming.

Some customers are friendly and quite talkative so be on your game to keep up whereas others can try and make your day worse by causing unnecessary complications and nuisances around the store.

You tend to learn how to handle and co-ordinate the older and the younger generation customers simultaneously as time goes on, but stay grounded as customers can change attitudes in a heartbeat if they do not get what they want or dislike their dining experiences. Your actions here will ultimately define your success in the short and long term as any mishaps can adversely affect your business reputation by the spreading of word of mouth.

Staff are the example you set to follow in terms of standards and delivery of quality and services to all guests so be careful not to dismiss the idea of further training to enhance and sustain all core standards and company procedures if required.

Abusive and violent customers should be dismissed promptly with caution as sometimes giving up and walking away is an option when the alternative is to suffer in any harms way. They clearly do not appreciate our efforts in consistently dedicating our time and resources in the making of goods and services; to then have to be abused or assaulted by customers. So, there is always an option to not give them any more satisfaction of your time and efforts.

Where some customers can become vain and envious in not accepting that sometimes customers can be at fault too as well as ourselves.

Staff can produce quality food and get home delivery sent out to customers in an instance but if the receiver mishandles the food upon opening and unpacking then surely it must be paramount that we are to blame? Hmm, debatable indeed.

We always should aspire to maintain a continuous reliable cycle of production and execution in a timely and effective manor for the sole purpose to help grow the business. But ultimately there are going to be negative bystanders looking to ruin your hard work and efforts along the way. Take any misjudgments or negativity as it comes and use it only to propel your drive to become even more successful.

I have been on both sides, as a customer and a business owner and can express profoundly the genuine exertion emphasis owners and staff instil in fulfilling customers every need and expectations is second to none.

Offering customers product discounts, samples and rewards is satisfactory as customers are happy they have saved and gained mutual respect and acknowledgement over their continued acts of purchases. Staff and management can feel satisfied also that they have accomplished their main objective in supplying the end user their befitting requests and thus help increase the business chances of growth and success at the forefront in the market industry.

We tend to allow ourselves to be stamped on our toes from customers with the slightest inconvenience occurring in business. It is just a small mistake, let it go and move on. Do not feel sorry for yourself, you are still learning aswell. We are all human and make errors from time to time. If you keep your foot out long enough someone is bound to trip or stamp on your toes, so keep yourself together, moving forward in tandem at all times and remaining professional in any circumstances that may arise.

Patience is a virtue, means absolutely nothing to customers when they are craving a sweet treat. The impending wait for satisfaction is an underlying trait many customers are not accustomed to. Every delay causes frustration but the quality installed in the production process will make all the wait worthwhile in the end.

Asking for feedback or how a customer has come to know of our business existence is a shrewd but very effective way to manage marketing strategies. A simple question and answer can point towards many avenues to exploit further, such as advertising on social media for instance. Find out if this is the method that the customer has gained awareness from and take note in the form of a results survey. Overtime, use the results to manage and ensure your general marketing strategy ploys are actually working and are positively getting you the results as intended.

We are not happy until you are happy! We do not stop until you are satisfied! We are united! We need each other to prosper and get what we want. We are equally seeking enjoyment. We are neither forceful nor irresolute in our engagements. We just ask for respect, as we are producing goods that you chose to forgo making yourselves at home so bare with us while we get it right!

Catering for customers is difficult but essential in the modern world where hospitality is increasingly becoming more of a challenge to grasp in such recent times of global pandemics.

Engaging in direct conversation can brighten ones day and a sense of feeling valued within. They may have had a bad day or morning so a short greeting and a smile can really do justice in the upping of ones spirits and mood. We are relieved to go the extra distance and to really connect with all our guests and thus leave a lasting impression.

Eventful Engagements

Below is a few highlights and fond memorable encounters with customers.

We all want to feel valued, we all want to be enjoying life to the max. Well stop looking and indulge in our delicious cookies. A good cookie can easily chip off any troubles one comes across and a taste to savour; for the many, not the few.

Tough Choice

Custard or chocolate sauce, now thats a decision to behold. Both have such elegance and texture but a sticky pudding situation calls for custard surely? A sponge calls for a douse of chocolate sauce surely? One is of no avail and equal to the other and with decisions like these, it can either make or break your customers day.

The Big Splash

Holding the waffle mix jug is not for the faint hearted. I only turned my back and splash bang wallop the waffle mix was all over the ceiling and surrounding walls. Slipped off the staff members hand apparently! No, it's not a load of waffle, honest!

Marshmallow Drama

Customers are always right? Right on your last nerves I reckon. Once a lady came along with around 10 kids straight from a local school, she had asked for a hot chocolate drink for one of the kids. Was made to order and served with passion as usual, all for the lady to express why there was no whipped cream, sprinkles or marshmallows on top for the kids to enjoy; as kids "love them extras."

Woah woah woah, we are not mind-readers now madam. Who gets a shouting at for not adding them extras on when they was not initially requested or even paid for, oh wait, me! As much as it seems hard to tell staff an order you would like initially, to then change forthcoming. That is fine, but what is not, is to patronise and downplay staff and our efforts in our initial opening week phase. There is a custom to commit a few errors on speed and transition to delivery so patience is a virtue while we get up to grasp with all our internal processes.

The stranger

I mean it is awesome when you have regular daily customers incoming, pleases us to see that we are actually offering and maintaining our quality products. One customer began to get so comfortable with their phone orders for collection, one day they ordered under my own name to which they found amusing and great banter. Just pick up your waffles and be on your way pal, waffling stays in the machine, its becoming Groundhog Day.

Happy one

Driving over 5 miles every weekend to get his sweet fix was no challenge for this person. Quickly becoming a regular around the place. We soon delivered out to them but they were always keen to come and see us to which was joyful.

Hundred and one

From a calm Sunday afternoon to bustling fanfare; a large crowd of supposedly same relative family and ancestors all had gathered in and outside the store. I mean the place could hold up to 40 at a push, but we was so overwhelmed all of a sudden. Making orders which we could one by one was easier said than done while maintaining store control. In a time of COVID-19 we would have been imprisoned for such an occasion.

Meet me halfway

He only came in for some gelato ice cream for his kids to savour, little by little he wanted a job. Or free ice cream who knows; hey, he only became a delivery driver. Legend!

Party Memories

Baby showers, birthdays, special anniversaries, all occasions were hosted and welcomed. The best times! Soon became a hotspot for the children too who never wanted to leave after such joyous experiences. That's what life is all about, enjoying and creating fond memories to look back on. FullEnjoyment

Late night sorrow

A Customer who got a text message that her friend had just passed away as they sat down to eat on a Late Saturday night; just 10 minutes before i was due to close. Yh I know what you are thinking. I cried inside also as they stayed longer! Sweet but bitter end to the evening for all.

The Fallout

A summer evening in June, I had left staff in charge as I was out attending a relatives 50th Birthday Party. Wasn't too long before untimely errors unfolded and I had to quickly regain control and summon staff to a meeting to discuss shortcomings. It was a time i realised that I could never get away from business life for any amount of short period. To say the least, I was just surprised the building was still standing.

Landlord from Hell

For a first time business venture, one would hope for smooth runnings, but not with a landlord from hell and back. Water leaks - shops flooding - electric wires wet - no responsibility taken. Stand-off after standoff, one should not purchase a property and then fall short of its responsibilities that come with it. Enough was enough!

Over-indulged

A group once had finished their desserts and stayed for a prolonged 3 hours after, chinwagging away until the sunset. I mean it is no issue to me, I like the idea that now I could play heads down thumbs up with a group. So there I go, I only pulled out the wrong finger and that was it. Enough, to see the back of them and off they went after getting the message, it was time to go.

Connections

On the upturn, many a times we had gestures of goodwill from our regular customers. A touch of class in offering some of their own business products or services for myself and staff to enjoy. Many a time fellow customers have initiated a proposal to combine businesses in a unique concept for the better good for end consumers to enjoy even more. Imported fair trade drinks, free of alcohol and sugar which the customer had recently tied up a big contract with American giant chain Walmart.

This was a very bespoke concept the customer had invented and thus duly trademarked his brand for safety of encroachment. A feature that would later take our business to the next level and ahead of competition. It is not what you know, its who you know. Opportunities will always come and go so be on guard to grasp the right choices and most achievable also to boost business fortunes and success.

My Heroes

Two friends who came in as guests were soon taking phone calls and orders as business quickly went manic. Was not long after delivery services commenced, and I was in and out on the road. They both stepped in and saved the day taking orders and payments while I was keeping up with deliveries. It was a call for more staff as demand was rising ever more.

Satisfied

We do not ask for tips, more for priceless feedback on how we are and what we could improve on. Little more than, oh keep the change. I mean save your pennies, why not leaves us a review for the experience you had with us instead. No pressure, just merely letting us know how the service and products you received turned out to be.

Dancing in the moonlight

One of the most remarkable and rememberable encounters was when three very joyful young ladies embraced our furniture by dancing the night away on tables and throughout the store. It was a bizzare but entertaining moment to witness, the puddings went down a treat that's all that could be said I guess.

Double Delight

You know you are doing wonders when you have customers who come instore to eat and then order for delivery later that exact same evening. Repeat the Treat, Twice as Nice, Double Trouble, call it what you will.

Damsel in distress

I myself upon a delivery drop, was ushered to join the party and take a break for a little while. As much as it was appealing, I politely refused and continued my deliveries. Apparently 50 shades of grey was on viewing inside, oh god what a shame that turned out to be!

The famous one

One makes you wonder what a telling business you behold when you are able to attract high calibre and renowned individuals to your setting. A striker for the Leicester City Fc, neither to say they had a sweet taste for our products, we certainly delivered to expectations and I even stroked lucky in getting a signed autograph picture of the two of us. Was definitely one special moment for the highlights reel which i can fondly look back on with joy.

Our doors are open for 10 hours at a time, serving all guests of different backgrounds and professions. Whether you are famed or not, everyone is treated equally and without prejudice. We aim to warm the hearts of our people and which they then return with more loved ones to enjoy a second, third, fourth time, that is our primary aim for all consumers we welcome through the doors.

Suppliers

They bring in the dirty work for all businesses to thrive on and become successful. A quality, reliable and cost effective supplier is above none else.

Negotiations are key in getting the best prices and products to offer customers. The discretion is important to keep close within the business and not allow a competitive advantage to others; not to leak out any relevant contracts or business dealings information with suppliers.

It is always okay to keep an eye for any new emerging suppliers entering the market as customer demands and market needs change over the years. We see a lot of Vegan and non dairy options at the forefront in retail supermarkets in recent times. So, there is a constant need to supply and deliver to customers every taste from time to time and a new supplier will not be the worst thing that you decide to take on.

Baring in minds the procurement and delivery logistics are kept in accordance with other current suppliers that the business utilises, this will allow operations to continue to run smoothly without any disruptions to the output of goods and services to the end consumer.

Believe it or not, one of my main suppliers got in touch with myself and by choice, a few months after we had opened. The owner himself got into contact and offered their services and a chance to come down instore and pitch their products to us. Now this is a supplier who are dominating in various supermarkets across the country. They also have a strong standing in Birmingham's main shopping centre with a string of kiosks and larger stores currently operating under their franchise.

They told us they really liked our brand appeal and what we were currently doing in the local area. Furthermore, wanting to partner with us in taking the business to the next step with their renowned quality Gelato ice cream range. Upon pitching their sample products to us, the range of taste and flavours was fantastic and really apparent to witness firsthand.

I was now very prompted to change from our current Gelato supplier. I believed for the benefit of the business growth and gaining a clear sense of stability in the fierce competitive market, i thus continued to participate in negotiating.

I had to negotiate hard with the owner himself who came down personally to meet us and represent his company. I found this to be a very significant period in my overall business experience. Let me stop for a minute, this person has chosen me and my business to aid and work alongside with a mutual aim in supplying customers the best quality available on the market. Is this real? Why me? Is this my business breakthrough? This is surreal.

I felt so grateful in them showing appreciation in what I was implementing in my company. Our vision was clearly evident and being in sync. After taking a brief moment to negotiate and haggle down a really befitting price range that suited my business, I decided it was ultimately the best decision to change supplier now.

In turn, we would have saved a lot in our supply and production costs so overall I was very happy I made the right choice. It was now or never. You have to always be ready for any approach from new suppliers and customs as the ever evolving growing market stops for no one as customer needs and wants change all the time. You either stick or twist for the business to prosper or fall short in potentially staying one step ahead of all competition.

My current Gelato supplier was informed of my decision in which they really pushed to keep our services. I politely thanked them for all their bespoke service and hospitality in the duration we was partnered together but the time was right to move on.

Tough decisions, tough personnel need to take and take alone. Let no one restrict or limit your decision making as you ultimately being the main business beneficiary, know what is best and what is not best for your own business. Any outside influences can be taken onboard but you yourself have to be strong and brave to make the final decision.

The relationship with the new supplier really took off and began to prosper into fruition relatively soon after we signed agreements. This is why it is key to always maintain a respectable and professional relations with all suppliers and they will help you and always be available in your time of need. Respect on both sides is unbreakable to thus being, we need them but they still need us in unison.

Staff

Staff or as I call it squaaaaad! Theres no I in TEAM but there is me in TEAM, and I am the squad alone. Just kidding we are all united and operate as a solid wholesome.

Enabling a management prerogative approach from the outset is also essential in signifying whose in charge. Not to mention reiterating the power to control the direction in which the business is heading in.

PRP culture – Polite, Respectful, Punctual

Polite in the greeting of all customers whether general public or family and friends that are entering the establishment; all guests are to be treated with the upmost decorum and with a smile

Respectful in maintaining that all guests are given the required privacy and comforts throughout the duration of their stay. Always being alert and available when called upon and staying cautious to any specific requests or changes to their meal or drinks.

Punctual to all work shifts in the correct uniform provided, abiding by the correct company policies at all times. Making sure to go above and beyond in providing the most satisfactory service and quality in food items that should also be served promptly.

Remunerations are crucial in keeping a young team of employees fully hungry and fired up to do and achieve more successes. Also continuously thriving to enable themselves to stand apart from direct competitors and to maintain overall employee retention.

A key way to maintaining employee retention is to set a series of small and achievable objectives over a period of set time which keeps the employee and management sustainable and continually developing skillsets simultaneously.

All customer tips must be handed to staff, as stated in our company policies. Hmm, this tip is heavy, surely policies can be amended right? I have nails to paint too and hair to maintain so I guess another tip bites the dust. Sshh! What they don't know, won't harm them, exactly! Minimum wage, Minimum Tips! Oh the joys of being in charge.

If your late, tell a mate. I don't do excuses nor sympathy so save the bother trying to explain yourselves. Like a biscuit takes to a cup of tea, is as quick and easy to set you free. If you Bunk, you gotta take the Dunk. A culture and principles are set install to obey and follow, do you want to jeopardise every other employee and operations because of one.

If a virus is growing and posing a threat inside the company, remove and replace it immediately to save further controversies and potential downfalls it could bring to the business. A late employee could lead to missed and late taken orders, all due to the negligence and competence of one individual. Act to restrict other employees having an option to follow suit or think this is acceptable, be ruthless if means must for the sake of the business.

But first always drop your own personal ego in making an important decision, it is not about yourself but the business as a whole first and foremost. Whether you liked the individual employee or not, this is not the time to reap the satisfaction to dismiss them from the workforce by pleasing your own accord. Later, this decision could come back to haunt you unjustly, so a careful but timely consideration is key to addressing any misconducts that may arise from employees.

Interviewing process of acquiring new personnel to add to the business organisation. Define what you are looking for, the relevant skills and experience new applications must possess. The needs of the business is key here, do not just try to fill a gap in the workforce for the sake of adding numbers when training new staff can become relatively costly and time consuming; without any means to actually help the business. Individuals must be aligned and in keeping with the management and ownerships vision.

Some employees merely work for the money, those others who show keen interests in the companies vision are the ones who are most adept and of significant value. A lot of times on interview, individuals will tell you what you want to hear. It is up to your own instincts to separate the truths from the flaws or lies you are being told. See, I follow a clear principle in life to that of, my instincts have never failed me, if you are still in contact with me, it is solely because I believe in you to succeed.

New individuals can and will inherit new traits at every new company they work for along their period of stay. Every business has its own unique approaches and working conditions so those candidates eager and motivated to strive and better themselves go further in being able to adjust accordingly and with relative ease.

Majority of my staff I took on in my business, were first time working with little to no prior experience. I felt that everyone needed to be given a chance to highlight their true potential and value in helping myself achieve profound success. You don't know how good someone is until they are given a chance or a springboard to showcase their talents.

Don't be afraid to take a risk as big as it may be, the rewards are also highly significant for all parties involved in their own right. We all need a chance right, someone is going to be the first to hire you one day eventually. So stay ready and focused to the end goal in gaining vital knowledge and experience on how the working environment operates whenever the opportunity comes along.

Best of both worlds:

An employee came in hungover for one shift, silly basic errors were a plenty and to which caused significant discomfort to customers and also a disruption to operations. Individual was sent home and summoned to a disciplinary meeting with immediate effect. I would rather cope with utilising less staff however busy we may be, than have any one individual contributing to any lasting errors. These errors can duly become unforgivable and cause profound affects in our reputation and communication. With customer service being to provide high level standards at all times a priority to our cultural setting.

A few treats for employees every so often is a good way in sustaining employee morale in addition to acknowledging their continued hard working efforts. Spontaneous team bonding events hosted from time to time is another means of praising employees and nurturing them in driving for more extended output. If you are on a par, level headed with your staff from the offset, knowing when to work and when to play, this is when business life is at its optimum enjoyment for all parties. Not just the after party's! They are FullEnjoyment!

Public Perception

What is perception at the end of the day. Do you care? Do you lose sleep at night because of careless remarks of others put upon you? Do you work to please others? Do you believe the public are in control of your destiny? Do you even have time to think like this, that's the question?

No matter what you do in life, if someone is going to take your actions the wrong way, albeit being morally acceptable, then this is clearly out of your hands and worrying about it is not going to help or even change their agenda they have against you. The theory being you can do any good deed in life, just for instance being nice and asking others how their day was, or if they are planning to do anything nice later on. This is just being friendly and part and parcel of your day job in customer service to all guests. It does not mean you want something in return. I mean outside of work it is a different matter entirely but that's not the point here.

It will always be the good, the bad and the ugly. The good are those who are the norm, being kind and polite out of courtesy. The bad are those who are rude and obnoxious upon customer engagement without any real reason to be. They have a grudge or ego they hold dear to themselves and in which they may be suffering to overcome. Let it not get to you, they will work it out themselves, one day bless them!

And finally the ugly being the ones that portray themselves to be pleasant and honest to your face but behind closed doors are insulting and bad mouthing you to others. Here again, let them say and do as they please, everyone else can see how you are. If you be yourself 99% of the time, the 1% will fall in place all in good time just like the others who are aligned to who and how you really are.

Sometimes people are quick to judge upon first impressions or engagements. I mean most of us can have a mean resting bitch face, but does not mean we do not want to have a chat about wether Donald trump wears a wig or not. I mean what is that barnet all about? You can share your thoughts, while I rest face!

I have been told I could be intimidating upon first glance, this is just the front cover, you ain't ready to read on yet it gets better. Honest! Most likely caught me in the mornings, then there becomes an issue. I will act like your not there. Who likes mornings anyway? Evening dessert times are the best am I not right? Call me then maybe!

You really do see who the real ones are when you are in the spotlight, not just in your time of need or low points in life. Just regulating the difference between a sense of meaningful desire to help make better a situation or being in smugness to merely watch you suffer in dire times. Those who just come to loaf and enjoy free products and services just because they think they have a right due to being an acquaintance.

A friend with benefits you may assume, that works both ways not one direction. You scratch our backs and we duly return the favour. Nothing is free in life other than having manners and respect for all. Pay as you go, or lose foul of your services just like your prized mobile networks. There is no extra credit for anyone, help our cause and in time you will gain recognised credit in the form of discounts and offers, but never a free hand.

If they really cared and supported you they would contribute like all others, as ultimately we have bills to pay too! They do not just pay themselves! Being able to self support and maintain a positive mindset is a mental challenge not many can handle the pressures of.

An outside support bubble or network around you can also enhance but not solely reliable in stability in both health and mental well-being. These are the times when you know who is coming to support, who is talking to come and support and those who only know what is going on through asking others but wont come and see for themselves.

Many, many, many persons that you initially thought were solid ambassadors of yours, only to become envious as they see you blossoming over time, it happens unfortunately as time goes on, people also change sadly.

Nobody wants to see you do better than them, only equal or less. No one flies your flag high in the sky other than yourself. You have to keep yourself flying high and above the rest of the misfortunate bystanders who want to see you fail. Sometimes giving a smile to your rivals can be so satisfying, they can not live with themselves. And will ridicule you all they want but do not let that stop you on your way to success and freedom from any negativity.

God is always watching aswell as those who believe in you and follow whether in spirt or physically, they too are right alongside you wishing you the upmost fortunes and unconditional love. Keep fighting until your last breath in any challenge you partake. Life is not easy, it is tough!

But the tougher you can make it, is by letting them win, stay ahead of the game and strike forward movements that no one can replicate. Life would be dull and boring if it was too easy, we need to keep ourselves in the right mindset and focused at all times as any given opportunity can arise at any time.

All opportunities are to be grasped and not dismissed quickly as you can always learn after as you go on but always take that chance now, it could be the one that you needed to change your life forever. You just wont know until you go for it, do not live the rest of your lives in regret. Time is short as it is, let us not waste any more moments that we could be encountering on wisely.

Competition

You are only as good as the next. The meaning behind this is that no matter how well established you are or concentrated in the current market, new entrants can sometimes simply start up and exploit opportunities in areas where you are currently lacking. To gain a foothold and potential market share ahead of you, there will always be someone in waiting to spoil your horizon and if they can help it, they certainly will.

This is why we need to be on guard and continually monitor and improve our efficiencies and operations including technology and processes to keep up with the latest trends and customer habits. One way to do so, would be to continue to invest in our very own people and staff to make sure we are well equipped in handling and preventing any possible disruptions that a new competitor could spring out of the unknown at any time. Improvement training and encouraging innovation amongst workforce are two possible methods to implement.

You can never be fully ready, but having a key risk management process and a stringent approach all the way throughout the hierarchy will help in controlling any potential threats in advance. Whereby managers are effective in mitigating risks, seeking opportunities to further enhance the companies status in becoming unique and collectively endeavouring new invention ideas and processes to stay aligned to the ever evolving needs and wants of our customers.

This attitude and belief should be aspired and duly forthwith instilled along the entire business pyramid top down, from the top CEO to directors/management and then all the way down to the lower workforce staff levels.

As an analogy, just like a dandelion blossoms from a seed to a beautiful yellow plant and then once fertilisation has taken place its new seeds, with the wind fly away to new areas and there, new plants are formed and the whole process starts again.

The lifecycle is continuous. This is how a business needs to have its missions and overall objectives continually monitored in ensuring they are still achievable, heading in the right direction and not on course to blow or fade away in essence and also if there any possible alterations that need to be made. These now known alterations should be completed as soon as possible as any rivals or competitors may be able to seek on these missed opportunities if any, to gain advantages if businesses do not act robustly.

I took an approach to undercut my local rivals on my initial start up pricing strategy, this led me to establishing an easy entrance gain and settling into the industry relatively smoothly. As profit margins on all items were considerably high, I was able to set lower selling prices than my nearest competitors without too many perpetuations on the ingredients cost prices.

Upon the first 6 months of my business opening a nearby sole delivering service for desserts only, soon packed in and moved on as we entered the market, they became unsustainable. The owner actually came down in person and offered me the business takeover outright to run alongside mine and reach more customers. I was contempt with my own new business runnings and simply replied, the customers will soon be ordering from us if they were not already, thanks but no thanks. I did it my way! And will continue to do so!

Now being the sole desserts business in the local town, this meant I had little direct competition but still needed to target a wider audience and put my business out further amongst the surrounding neighbourhoods and cities, in order to expand. Every single new entrant into the market is always a threat no matter what you say to yourself or how well established you currently are. For some new entrants the potential is so huge they can rise and be on a par in no time, so never let your foot of the gas and remain in a strong position using methods previously mentioned earlier.

At the end of the day, there are always many sharp robust thorns along the stem of a bright red rose. Think, I am now the becoming of that top Rose flower. The rest will duly be on the same path (stem) however as I continue to grow, I bypass all thorns (competitors) to reach closer to the sunlight where I will be free in standing alone, to now absorb all the rewards.

Find your happy medium, in utilising best suited marketing methods that are designed to push your company to greatness and set you apart from the rest.

The race is one! Start as you mean to go on! Some will cut corners to get one over on you, any industry can be a vicious demanding market with ever changing customer habits.

I can frankly say a lot of competitors do deceive their customers in their advertising and marketing strategies in portraying items in ways that seem too good to miss out on. That is their job as they want to gain more custom, to gain more money, it is a one dimensional focus for them, but yours is to see where you would in fact benefit out of all this.

Nowadays, the mainstream social media networks are becoming increasingly popular with the emergence of well known so called global influencers who amass a large social following. These influencers are effective techniques used to promote products and services around the world to different demographics on behalf of a company in exchange for personal gifts or money.

Do not be fooled as products are not always as transparent as they seem to be shown, so be ready to be disappointed. An ever growing list of influencers are becoming brainwashed and an increased self of worth or living made out of others and their business needs and desires.

Think of this like an actor (influencer) and director (company) in which they are directed to do as they are told so the film looks all well and good for its viewers to divulge and enjoy. Act on intelligence as it is easy to be pulled into different schemes as they look good on filters, just because they work for others does not mean you will benefit from the same.

Be your own boss! Influence yourself!

Investors

What are they bringing to the table?

What are the intentions?

Are you really ready to give up a part stake or whole of what you have worked so hard to build, was that always the aim from inception?

Do not be quick to jump to an agreement and give everything up, take your time and decide on the best potential candidates.

Draw on your instincts and summarise the pros and cons of introducing a new partner or a whole sale of business.

Asking for advice from your friends or family members may be wise but ultimately the final decision will solely rest on your shoulders.

Sometimes investors want to come in and change a great deal which could cause an impact to the overall business structure including staff personnel and at other operational levels.

Trust is a mark of someone's integrity which would require investors to be upfront and not lead you into a fairytale and promise you something that would clearly be naive and non sensical in ever being successful in joining forces with yourself.

If you feel doubts or any gut feeling that you are not contempt with, then make it known as early as possible and do not waste anymore time or disclose any more business information to others than is absolute necessary.

Critical business information would initially need to be disclosed to potential investors to entice them to make an offer, how much you disclose is solely dependent on what you feel is acceptable as you do not want to overindulge someone with unnecessary information which could put them off or on the other hand not disclose too much fine details on business operations which others can then easily replicate and possibly soon become your arch nemesis. That is then another competitor to worry about, you do not want that if you can help it.

I had offers whereby a group of investors would come in and implement wholesome changes from store set-up to food menu choices and overall compensating half of my original menu. I would go off in the meantime and oversee the whole business from afar and then duly return when the new changes were in full force after a few months.

This was a risky move and non practical in my mind. Our business was already established and if anything, needed to be branched out or another range of hot food items added beside original full menu for all our current and potential new customers to devour. You should not change drastically even if someone is painting a Da Vinci art piece in front of you.

Most people are in it for themselves, in the sense that a lot of people struggle and cannot initially start a business from an idea themselves so they are out there waiting and searching purely for investment opportunities.

Just remember everything we, ourselves invest in whether purchasing clothes, food, cars, houses, anything as such, it is only to benefit yourself so when an investor comes along their sole aim is to see and find what can they alone benefit from, from you and your idea or concept.

Have your wits about you!

Happiness in health over happiness over money

Are you killing yourself everyday trying to make a living?

Are you money motivated and driven?

Are you able to enjoy your life and spend time with your family and friends?

If you died tomorrow would you take your money or wealth with you. I'm all for the strategy of you only live once but… only within limits. These limits should have a sense of control where you do not put yourself in any harms way by endangering yourself attempting to make a living or even over indulging spending your earnings.

It takes only one error for everything to come crashing down, so always think twice, is it worth it. Do not be selfish as others around you will become embroiled in your demise by your lack of judgement. There is no respawn or restart button in life. We are not in a gaming world, we should not bet on our lives or futures for nobody.

Having made more money than I had forecasted in my first business, this did not make me happy. I was so fatigued and I could not think anymore. I needed a break but a break in business is not a given, if you do not have the right cover or trust in place, you can not ever have a break or work remotely even.

My health is important for my long term future, I am still so young, I want to be free and live for another day before something serious happens to my deteriorating health. Making it known that there will be times where you just can not sit down to enjoy a normal meal, you can not reply back to everyone, you can not always freely even go to the toilet, at any time or catch some air outside once in a while, you have to give up a lot to really make your business a success from a start up alone by yourself. You have to be on your game every minute, every hour of the day, 80 or 90 hours a week, all year round. It can take its toll on anyone!

Having a partner or other support from staff assistants, can maybe provide more opportunities for rest and comfort breaks but the case remains the same, can some cover you and perform the same as you and with equal consistency on a day to day basis with the methodology you have driven to kick start the business from. The short answer to this is no, hence the purpose of me calling time on my business was that handing a duty to anyone to takeover the store and run the business without me, it takes one small mistake and everything can collapse. It is my sole responsibility, my staff have their own focus in life so it is too risky and unfair to place a burden on them and for all the years of me building reputation up to end in minutes. So, therefore it can only be me who fails and if I am ever going to go then everything has got to go with me and be closed entirely.

It is not in my nature to shy away from making such decisions, as I have had to make more important personal decisions previously which gave me confidence in handling this exit well both mentally and physically.

There is no passover, it started with me and it ends with me on my own accord, I believe this is how it should be. A short term loss in closure equates to a long term gain in my prosperity and freedom. I have completed my biggest dream, no one can take that away from me ever. My health is paramount and without me at full capacity nothing will be the same. It is easy to say just get a manager in charge and meanwhile go and do something else. I think once you do this the stress amps up another level with vigorous overlooking and making sure all operations are running to upmost optimum. The control is now in someone else's hands, do you want added stress or lack of awareness that your policies and procedures are still going to be intact with you not in attendance as much.

Freedom is very undervalued in life, as such when we have no responsibilities to be concerned about, an ease of calmness in roaming any path without stipulations and anxiety, together retaining a sense of comfort; we can then timely when ready, seek the next opportunities or direction in our life.

Having huge amounts of money or living a lavish lifestyle does not faze me or attract me in any way or sense. If you are not fit and healthy enough to enjoy your money then there becomes zero value on health.

If you encounter any health defining symptoms or incidents while trying to maintain your intense work rate then this could inturn vastly affect your long term wellbeing. It is okay to let go for the greater good. Live on for another day, and in time go again. If we held on to everything and anything long enough we could easily endanger ourselves and even endanger the potential growth of a business more importantly. There is no shame or repercussions to admitting a loss to fortunes in the short term as in life nothing is determined or guaranteed to last forever so dwindling on this is unnecessary as in one year or two or five years down the line you could easily be back in a comfortable, healthier environment.

I am more than content with the bare minimum, we can all take on methods to amass our fortunes but at what cost to show for them. I, as I have been all my life chasing and completing my dreams one by one as soon as I am able to, have profound self-satisfaction and found comfort in that I have done it the right way and most importantly "My Way".

Leaving Legacy

Since the young age of 5, Every one person who has come to pass through my life, i have told them that they will never come across anyone like me in their entirety. Not to take this as being arrogant or anything as such, merely being totally confident in my nature and abilities that I was meant to be out of the ordinary and apart from the rest.

Never once boasted about anything i have achieved in the past or achieving now, i just wont stop until god lifts my arm in the air in the end life and only then will i know i made it. Never claimed to be something i am not, talk less and show more is the way. When it matters most the job always gets done.

My capabilities are second to none and my mind forthcoming is untouchable to any element. This dream first business was just starters, what I do next will be bigger and better, that will always be my way of becoming the best I can possibly be with a resolute mindset. I have lost the single most important person of my life at a tender age, I was not afraid, I was brave, I was stubborn to fulfil my dreams all by the age of 22. I am now privileged and blessed to be in such position of tranquility and prosperity to tell of my thoughts and wisdom to even a select few that are reading on.

Not many people are accustomed to coming to terms with why I am who I am and why I do the things I choose and want to do, hopefully they will gain a better understanding and recognition reading my insights and in turn acquire some knowledge and lessons to take for themselves.

Those who want to follow and copy suit and pretend they can replicate any of my accomplishments. Of course it is possible and I wish them well, but focus on your own means of life and journey. I would want my child striving to be better and set the bar higher than I have done. My aim would be for them to learn and understand the lessons I learnt throughout my life and grasp opportunities with both hands as they come to them. Only then will they become to realise the true means of a role model.

Let us aspire to idolise ourselves first and foremost. Make brave and freestanding choices that you are comfortable with and create your own history. Leave a legacy and etch your name in the history books for all to witness. A door is always within an eye sight away, it is only upon yourself to rise up and open that door to start your next adventure. Do not leave it too late, those who have accomplished their dreams at a later stage in life have always regretted that they never made an earlier move at a young age.

Where there is a will, theres an entitlement passed down to you from family inheritance or likewise. Some are happy to have things handed to them and thus carry on family traditions. This is perfectly okay if it becomes of the best interests in the family to carry on the legacies of those members who have come before them in establishing such an affluent wealth to live on long into the future.

This is where you have to carry the mantel or decided to sell the business on to make a quick fortune. If your feel incapable of being able to handle those pressures of controlling the business entity, find some help and at least try, do not give up without trying. You already lost then, winners win by virtue of putting their entire mind, resources and passion in their vigorous approach to glory.

It is not always about establishing fortunes, if you are not happy doing what you are currently doing. Then it is perfectly acceptable to place others, albeit expert fielded professionals to carry the business holdings in a corporate executive position.

An exceptional benefaction of gifting or donations to charitable causes you have supported or are in support of is a incredible act of generosity and a selfless devotion. We need to support one another in our time of need, you never know when you will need a helping hand, so be nice and cautious in staying true to yourself. At the same time, in not always dismissing anyone or everyone who comes into your life. One day they may be the only person around you that could aid you in your desperate time of need.

Some of our loved ones are taken too early from us, we therefore persist on continuing their legacy for the foreseeable. A charity or foundation set up as a means to raise awareness of such loss and conditions that you wish to help others understand and hopefully seek help in advance. This is fantastic and very thoughtful tradition many people partake in, the loved ones are dearly remembered and in time become an icon in their own respect. Unfortunately, at times we do not deserve our loved ones and only realise when it is too late. So be sure to cherish every possible engagement and experience blissful memories whenever possible which you can look back on fondly without any regrets.

Let us take a moment of silence to remember all those loved ones we have lost. I wish and pray that you get the peace all in good time and that you retain hope and happiness within yourself, they are never too far away.

There will be many more opportunities to come my way in the future where I will be looking to enhance on my legacy and leave an everlasting effect on my fellow peers, friends and family. And in doing so, seek the uppermost satisfaction along the way.

Aftermath and Future

Risk

What type of risk person are you?

Risk averse, this is where you shy away or are not as keen to pursue a risk regardless of the rewards waiting on the other side.

Risk neutral is satisfied with both being a risk seeker and also avoiding taking risks, albeit depending on the circumstances placed upon them.

Risk seeker, someone who likes to take risks and is even willing to pay for it, also known as risk lover.

Knowingly, this determines your way of judgement and attitudes in the approach of a course of nature or event that is beyond your normal control.

What is your appetite to risks?

Are you prone to avoiding opportunities that you put off and which later become challenges; potentially you feel guilt or regret in the sense that perhaps the opportunities foregone could have been a catalyst in revolutionising your future.

How much are you prepared to tolerate as an individual, are you hungry or content?

Consider this in any future occurrence that passes by, sooner rather than later, do not let yourself hold any more burdens for the rest of your lives. Let's risk it for more than a biscuit.

You should identify the current risks that affect you in day to day life. For instance, if you do not complete something on time or keep to an arrangement, what would be the repercussions or consequences from this. This could be for example, adhering to a car insurance policy or meeting a coursework deadline on time.

Will you get another chance?

Overtime, as you grow older, your attitude, appetite and tastes as well as your beliefs, will evolve and so might your ascendancy to risk taking albeit whether you become more risk averse or even risk seeking more frequently, depending on your circumstances at the time and stage in life.

For myself, I will continue being a risk seeker in the future as I set myself new goals to aspire towards. I am content with putting myself out of my comfort zone and going above and beyond to really fulfil my potential to the maximum. However, I would only do so if the rewards are justified and not putting myself or others in a dangerous position in the process.

My next goal and dream that I am currently working towards is my ACCA Chartered Accountant membership, which I have a few exams left to complete. Accountancy has always been my main profession and undoubtedly the time has come to finish what I had started before my business adventures. Looking further ahead I intend to open my own Accounting firm whether in the UK or abroad.

Having a new focus in life is just what we need and it becomes a prerogative for our progression to ultimate self-enjoyment and self-success. Knowingly we can make wise decisions and plans around a main focus which all inter-align with one another albeit holiday plans, events and special occasions, investment opportunities or saving for investment into property, cars etc.

This all starts with one aspect, are you willing to risk to reach the promised land? The gold pot at the end of the rainbow is a myth but the risk for valued rewards for a better becoming is a priceless virtue that one should not shy away from.

The promised land is of what you make of it, brainstorm and visualise with a long term approach of a vision board perhaps, which details and outlines the elements and targets you wish to meet by a specified period of time.

Also, along the path, express what you wish to gain or acquire, whether properties, investments in stocks or shares or even a business idea you wish to embark on one day. This will set you well on your way with a total focusing aim and provide daily motivation when you see the vision board every morning before you leave your home.

Each one of our journeys are all unique and defined by our own individual creativity and designed to enhance our experiences to make the most out of our lives.

Your sports supercar does not define that you are more successful than others.

Your designer belt on your waist is not the Only belt to hold up your trousers.

Your smart phone is not the only format of communications.

These are luxuries! First conform to the essentials that are most vital for the foundations and creation of our aspirations and dreams.

We gather the essentials, we conquer our dreams, we gain satisfaction and enjoyment. Straight process!

If we have opportunities for luxuries along the way then so be it but these are not essentials; that start the process over and over again.

Luxury goods wear out and move away from you over time. Our essential tools such as knowledge, experience and self beliefs go untouched and stay with us forever which no one can take from you.

Sharpen your tools prior to embarking on a new journey!

Choices are part and parcel in life, no choice is right or wrong. Mistakes are to be made for our lessons to be learnt. Experiences are good or bad. All to which shape your views and focus in life that in the future your "Decisions" that you take on become unilateral to what you have witnessed and congregated in past situations so that you are now at a greater good in being successful in any future ambitions.

I hope in the future to travel a lot more to other avenues around the world, learning about new cultures and understanding how others chase and live out their dreams also. Travelling is a unique experience to witness new horizons and create lasting memories with fellow loved ones and friends.

Whether we witness historical landmarks like the seven wonders of the world, sunny beach resorts, many different sports and leisure activities such as snowboarding on the french alps to jet skiing along Miami Beach. These are some of the things on my bucket list I wish to see and attempt in the future.

I continue to keep myself grounded and in doing so I am able to achieve the objectives and goals I set before me in a timely manner. I say time is taken for granted and our essence is life, so let's get out there and get things done!

Find the real you in you and not the you you want people to falsely pretend who you are. Believe in your inner sanctuary that anything you set your mind to is possible and not take no for an answer!

Oh,
Written in the stars
A million miles away
A message to the mane
Oh,
Seasons come and go
But I will never change
And I'm on my wayyy!

Quotes

"Once you realise your true value in life, you will then be able to do things that others can only sit and dream about" - #ITK

"One day my story will come into focus And they won't be just listening, they'l be taking f*cking notes" RS

"Never forget those that helped you get to where you are today, whether that was big or small" - Numero Uno

"Everything happens for a reason only when that one reason can make everything happen"
- The undeniable

"Wearing your heart on your sleeves can go both full or half hearted in expressing emotions" - Sleeveless

"Don't Judge anyone on their features, Judge anyone on their intellect" - Mind Over Matter

"The difference between a smart one and a blessed one is that one came up with gifts and one came down with a gift" - Almighty

"The first thought in your head is whether you take that risk to success or think twice in regret" - Risk seeker

"Self motivation above all separates the strong from the weak, a key element in any situation" - You are special

"What is meant to be will be but in the times when things are not meant to be, this will determine your understanding on eternity as nothing is forever" - Gods Will

"Never be afraid to speak the truth, if they are hurt by it, good they'l learn something for next time" - Speak Up

"Being in control is a comfort that opens up limitless opportunities of self-esteem" -In hand

"Giving up is an option when the alternative is to suffer in any harms way" - Let go

"They say the best come but once in a lifetime" - Finest

"Trusting the real ones is where if the shoe was on the other foot would they do the same you would do for them" - Trust Issues

"Sometimes it's best to just be living in the moments and not cameras" - No filter

"Got me a whole lotta honey...now even the bees envy me" - Sweet One

"There's a fine line between arrogance and confidence" - Same same but different

"My Instincts never failed me, If you are still In contact with me, It Is because I believe In you" - The chosen ones

"They say life Is too short, too short In the real ones" - Limited

"Freedom Is the most underrated aspect In life" - Let Breathe

"Never mistake my kindness, It's not a matter of wanting something In return, that Is just my nature" - Kind

"Surround yourself with different people, whether older or wiser as this will broaden your knowledge and heighten your understandings of life" - Wise Guy

"Never be afraid of being out of your comfort zone, It's the best possible way to enhance your abilities and experience life to the fullest"

"Keep your enemies at arms length, keep your loved ones hand In hand"

"People come and go, some go forward with you whilst others are left behind chasing your shadows"

"Trust can be broken and fixed, with a matter of forgiveness but without forgetting"

"We don't talk enough nowadays...we want to read captions rather than embrace ones chin wags"

"Your haters are always watching...with popcorn and a drink In hand waiting for you to fail; keep the adverts going"

"Customers are always right...right on your last nerve"

"Being In charge Is not a matter of coincidence, It's a matter of skill that you earn 't"

"Nowadays people see taking time out for others as more of a desperation than only contacting one when in dire needs or help"

"A helping hand can reinvigorate your Inner desire to continue on through any hardship"

"Push harder than you did yesterday If you want a different tomorrow"

"They told me I couldn't. That's why I did It"

"The one who plants trees, knowing that he will never sit In their shade, has at least started to understand the meaning of life"

"You can't beat me, I made this game"

"Here for a good time, not a long time"

"Dream chaser, stubborn to succeed, plan meticulously, no limits, adapt to difficulties, strive for perfection" - I Did It My Way

Meanings and lessons learnt on my journey through life's experiences

Of course you will make mistakes, but not trying would be the biggest one.

Sometimes you just have to disconnect and enjoy your own company. Let no one get In the way for a time, while you get back to a good standing and at peace. Self enjoyment Is a key to achieving your success and fortunes won't advocate for relying on others for this purpose of enjoyment. It starts with you, you have to love yourself first and foremost before anyone else.

It eventually gets better, without any sort of explanation; one day you just realise that you're no longer upset. You're no longer mad, hurt, or bothered by the things that took so much of your energy and thoughts.

You will then find yourself In a peaceful place and really hold on to that feeling.

Sometimes in life the hardest pill to swallow is learning that no matter how good you could be to someone, no matter how much you love them, they can and will turn their back on you.

Discipline Is one of the strongest forms of self-love. It Is Ignoring current pleasures for bigger rewards to come. It Is loving yourself enough to give yourself everything you have ever wanted.

You need three hobbies In life:

1. To keep you creative

2. To keep you In shape

3. To make you money

A big lesson I learnt this past year is that, you are not always going to get the closure or the explanation you think you deserve. Sometimes you have to accept something for what it is, and move on. Everything really does happen for a reason.

Over many years I have been chasing after people and being the only one trying to fix everything, it does become physically and mentally exhausting. I have to stop and find peace with whoever comes and goes In my life. Don't be the only one putting In effort because you will ultimately lose yourself trying to save someone else.

I have become my own hero at such a young age In accomplishing all my goals and dreams, I now need to set more goals and continue to dream vividly.

Everyone Is quick to criticise, let's see you get up and go commit and dedicate yourself to run a successful business by age of 22. Are you brave enough? Brave enough to criticise and nothing else!

Social media Is a tool that Is used to fool you. People with 10,000 followers or likes are still lonely as hell and that of another person with just 10 have plenty of friends. People who don't post pictures of themselves and their significant others, but are still In a beautiful loving relationship. People who are up to their neck In debt yet live and boast lavish Instagram lifestyles. Remember, this Is not real life. Appearances are just that...appearances.

Getting out of your comfort zone as soon as possible will feel scary but will ultimately bring out the best In you. Revealing untouched personal skills and traits you never knew you had. This Is how we grow, so whenever It feels scary to jump, that Is exactly when you jump. Otherwise you end up staying In the same place your whole life and regrets will grow Instead of potentials.

Remain positive and humble foremost yourself always, whether others around you are not aligned to your status, morals or beliefs. One must let go and keep distant from negativity anywhere or anytime throughout your life.

People want to put a spin against what we achieve and downplay our accomplishments because they are envious and cannot replicate. It Is not your fault, Ignore them and keep yourself and your important close ones grounded and In positivity. This Is the ultimate satisfaction and self-motivation one can ever have and such to continue on your merry way In achieving more successes In your future endeavours.

Overthinking Is a killer and can really suppress your feelings and attitudes down, to which you begin to struggle to communicate and behave as effectively as you first wanted to. Thinking over things and aspects that have happened or may not happen, Is pointless and very draining. Follow your gut and go with a sense of trust In yourself and don't look back or even too far ahead.

Always trust your gut Instincts, they tend to be right 99% of the time. Having done so, you are less likely later on to feel remorse or guilt In not following what was beholding within you.

Following head over heart can be a relief as you can easily become blinded by what you feel you need, to that of what you already have. If you feel you need comfort, you have family and friends or even professionals to seek.

Seeking a new companion or partner just for the sake of filling a void In your life can be foreseen, as you already have what you need In family so let It not be mistaken or get lost In your ways. You could easily hurt yourself or others for using and abusing others just to seek parity and comfort for short times.

It is often said that a lie can get halfway around the world while the truth is still putting its shoes on.

Highlights

167

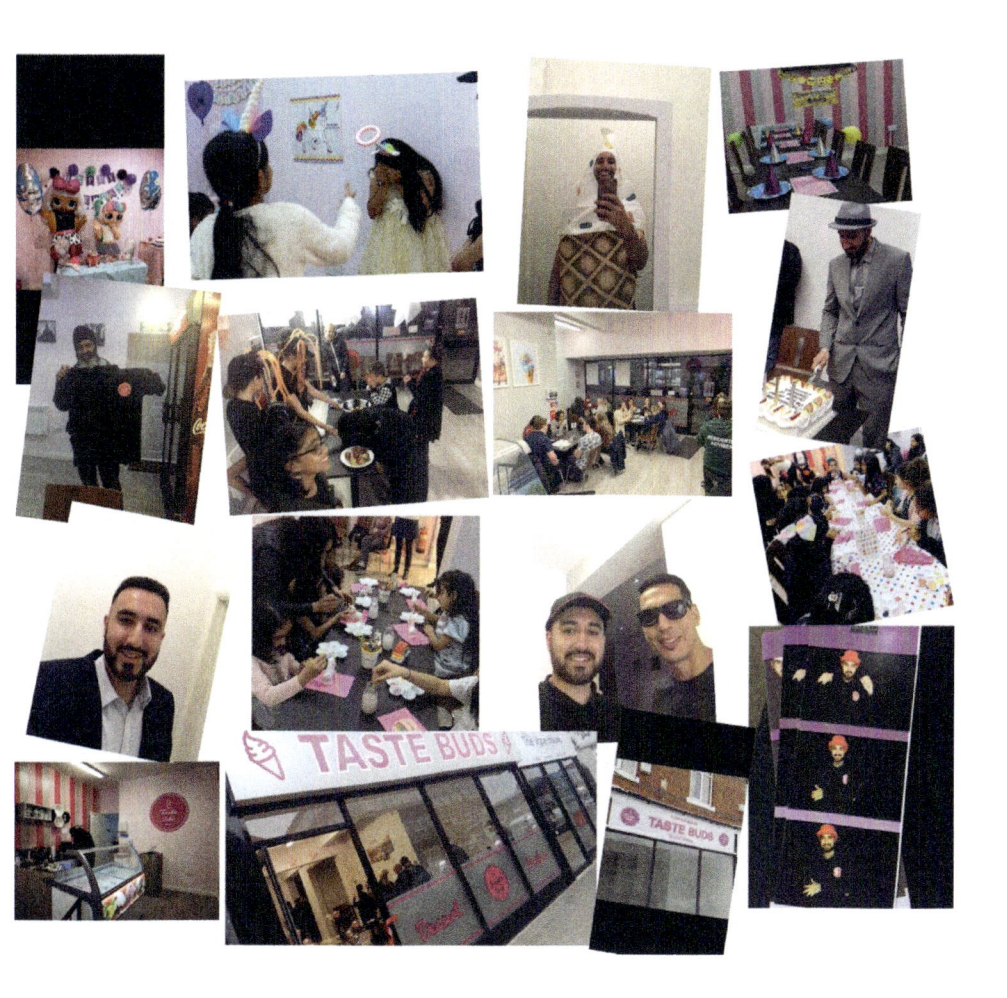

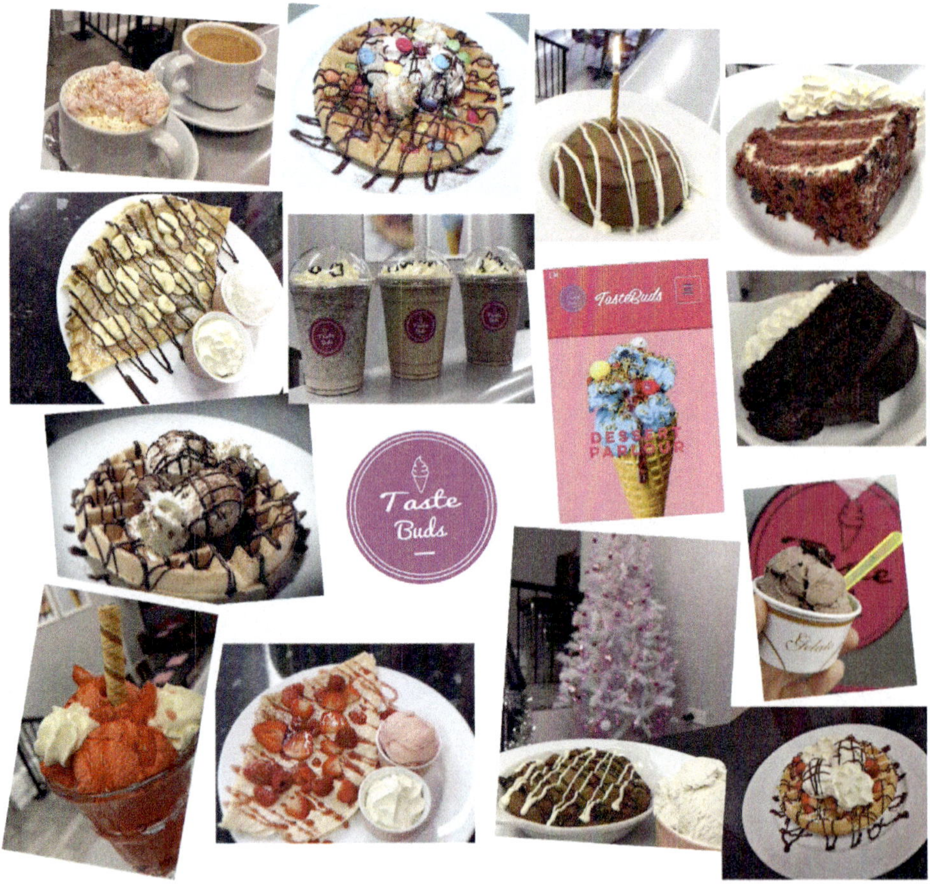
TasteBuds
Taste
Buds

169

K.H	P.P	J.G
R.P	D.K	M.S
I.L	H.K	S.D
M.M	A.S	L.G
A.N	J.H	H.G
M.E	M.D	N.P
S.N	T.S	H.S
E.D	K.K	A.M

THANK YOU
FOR EVERYTHING

Printed in Great Britain
by Amazon